..... Kids-Life .....

# BIBLE

Chariot Books is an imprint of ChariotVictor Publishing
A division of Cook Communications, Colorado Springs, Colorado 80918
Cook Communications, Paris, Ontario
Kingsway Communications, Eastbourne, England

THE KIDS-LIFE BIBLE
© 1998, 1994 by Educational Publishing Concepts, Inc., Wheaton, IL.
Exclusive distribution by Chariot Books.

Previously published as *The Kids-Life Bible Storybook.*

First hardcover printing, 1994
First paperback printing, 1998
Printed in Singapore
02  01  00  99  98      5  4  3  2

# Kids-Life
# BIBLE

## Mary Hollingsworth

*Illustrated by*
**Rick Incrocci**

Kingsway Publications
Eastbourne

# Old Testament Stories

Dear Parents .......................................................................... 10

God Made Our World *Gen. 1:1-23* .................................... 11
God Made People *Gen. 1:24-31* ...................................... 18
Snake In the Garden *Gen. 3:1-24* .................................... 23
Rain, Rain, Rain *Gen. 6:9–7:16* ...................................... 31
Noah's Family Is Saved *Gen. 7:17–9:29* .......................... 37
God's Promise To Abram *Gen. 15:1–17:5* ........................ 42
Isaac-Son and Sacrifice *Gen. 21:1-5* ............................... 48
Jacob Tricks Esau *Gen. 25:29-34* .................................... 53
Joseph, A Kind Brother *Gen. 37–45* ................................ 59
Moses Is Born *Exod. 2:1-10* ............................................ 65
A Burning Bush *Exod. 3:1–4:17* ...................................... 72
Walking Through the Sea *Exod. 14:10-31* ........................ 78
Moses Talks To God *Exod. 19:1–20:21* ............................ 84

Rahab Helps God's Spies     *Josh. 2, 6*......................................91
Jericho's Walls Fall Down     *Josh. 6*........................................98
Deborah Leads God's Army     *Judg. 4:1-16*.........................105
Samson, The Strongest Man     *Judg. 13:24; 16*..................110
Ruth, A Loyal Woman     *Ruth 1—4*.......................................116
God Hears Hannah's Prayer     *I Sam. 1:1—2:11*.................121
Saul Becomes King     *I Sam. 9:15—10:24*...........................126
David and the Giant     *I Sam. 17*...........................................132
Two Good Friends     *I Sam. 18—20*.......................................139
Three Mighty Men     *II Sam. 23:13-17*..................................144
God's Temple     *I Kings 5—6*..................................................151
Wise King Solomon     *I Kings 10:1-10*..................................158
Elijah Rides a Whirlwind     *II Kings 2:1-15*.........................163
Elisha and the Pot of Oil     *II Kings 4:1-7*...........................169
Joash, The Boy King     *II Kings 11:21—12:16*......................174
Brave Queen Esther     *Est. 2—5*.............................................179
The Shepherd's Song     *Psalm 23*..........................................185
Three Men In a Fire     *Dan. 3:1-30*.......................................191
Daniel and the Lions     *Dan. 6:1-28*.....................................197
Jonah Runs From God     *Jonah 1—4*....................................203

# New Testament Stories

Mary and the Angel      *Luke 1:26-38*.................................209
Jesus Is Born      *Luke 2:1-7*.................................213
Shepherds Visit Baby Jesus      *Luke 2:8-20*.................................218
Wise Men Bring Gifts      *Matt. 2:1-12*.................................225
The Boy Jesus      *Luke 2:40-52*.................................233
John Baptizes Jesus      *Matt. 3:13-17*.................................241
Jesus Teaches the People      *Matt. 5–7*.................................246
Jesus' First Miracle      *John 2:1-12*.................................251
Jesus Chooses Twelve Helpers      *Mark 3:13-19*.................................257
A Little Boy's Lunch      *John 6:1-15*.................................262

Jesus Walks On the Lake  *Matt. 14:22-33*......................................269

A Blind Man Can See  *John 9:1-12*..............................................276

A Good Man Stops to Help  *Luke 10:25-37*.................................281

A Lost Son Is Found  *Luke 15:11-24*..........................................288

A Poor Woman's Gift  *Mark 12:41-44*........................................294

The Last Supper  *Luke 22:7-20; I Cor. 11:23-26*.......................299

Soldiers Arrest Jesus  *Mark 14:32-50*........................................305

Jesus Dies  *Matt. 27:32-61; Mark 15:16-47*...............................310

Jesus Lives Again  *Matt. 28:1-10*...............................................318

Jesus Goes Back to Heaven  *Acts 1:6-12*...................................325

The Holy Spirit Comes  *Acts 2*...................................................330

Beggar at the Beautiful Gate  *Acts 3:1-10*.................................336

Seven Servants Chosen  *Acts 6:1-7*............................................343

A Nobleman Is Saved  *Acts 8:26-39*..........................................348

Saul Meets Jesus  *Acts 9:1-22*....................................................353

Dorcas Lives Again!  *Acts 9:36-42*.............................................358

God Saves Cornelius' Family  *Acts 10:1-48*...............................364

Paul Travels for God  *Acts 13:1-3—14:8-15*..............................370

Jesus Will Come Again  *Rev. 1:1-3; 21:1—22:21*.......................378

# Dear Parents,

Teaching our children the principles of God's Word is a wonderful and important activity. It's important for building character so that as they grow older, our children can become the people God meant them to be.

But the Bible is not just a book to help us in the future. It is a practical, hands-on instruction book for today. It can teach kids—even little ones—how to deal with problems they face every day at home, at school, at church, . . . everywhere.

The challenge then becomes: How can we convey these important biblical truths to our children?

The *Kids-Life Bible* will help you reach that goal, whether you are a parent, grandparent, teacher, or friend. Each story is followed by Kids-Life Questions that will help your child apply the Bible truth to his or her own life. This element is key to continued Christian growth—applying the Bible to a kid's life today.

You are the key. As you read each story, the Bible will come alive. Your child will discover that the Bible tells us about real people who struggled with the same issues we do today: *Will God be there when I need Him? Can I trust Him to supply my needs? Is God my friend? How should I treat my friends?. . . my parents?. . . even those I don't like, as well?*

As a result, we know that new opportunities will open up to you as you share the Bible together. What a wonderful investment you are making in the future of your child!

*Mary Hollingsworth*

# God Made Our World

*Genesis 1:1-23*

In the beginning was our wonderful God. Our world was empty. Everything was dark and gloomy. So, God decided to make our world a happy place for us to live.

*11*

God told the light to shine brightly. And FLASH! Beautiful light chased the darkness into night. God called the light *day* and the darkness *night*. That was the first day and night.

**O**n the second day God made air. We call it *sky*. The sky is a space so big and high and wide that it has no end.

13

Wonderful things happened on the third day! God made bubbling streams and sparkling seas. He planted golden wheat, apple trees, and grape vines. Then He smiled because it was all very good.

The fourth day was exciting, too! God hung the big warm sun in the day sky. And He hung the silver moon and glittery stars in the dark sky as night-lights for the world.

On the fifth day God had fun making fishes and birds. He made angel fish, catfish with long whiskers, and pretty rainbow trout. He made squawking parrots, pink flamingos, and ducks that waddle and quack. It was a good day!

# Kids Life QUESTIONS

1. What was the world like before God started making things?

2. Which day did God make the sun and the moon?

3. What pets have you had that God made?

## FUN & FACTS

Did you know that God put a special springy cushion behind the beak of a woodpecker? It's like a shock absorber that helps the woodpecker peck all day and not get a headache! Isn't God wonderful?

# God Made People

*Genesis 1:24-31*

God worked hard on the sixth day making animals. He made puppy dogs and kitty cats and kangaroos. He made furry rabbits and prickly porcupines, giant elephants and tiny hamsters.

Finally, God made people! He made a man named Adam and a woman named Eve. He told them to have children and to take care of His world.

God gave Adam and Eve grain for food. He gave them apples, grapes, bananas, and oranges to eat. And He gave them green plants to feed the animals and birds. God always takes care of His people.

Everything God had made was very good. And God smiled because He had finished making the world. Then on the seventh day, God rested.

# Kids Life QUESTIONS

1. What two jobs did God give Adam and Eve?

2. What did God do when He finished making the world?

3. What is something you can do to help Adam and Eve take care of God's world?

## FUN & FACTS

God covered most of the world with dirt. And it is wonderful! Soil feeds the plants we eat. Jewels, like diamonds, are found in the ground. Ants and worms and other insects have their homes underground. God even made people out of dust! Isn't God amazing!

# Snake in the Garden

*Genesis 3:1-24*

God let Adam and Eve live in a beautiful garden called Eden. In the evening God would come and walk in the garden. Adam and Eve would talk to God. He was their Friend.

God told Adam and Eve they could eat fruit from every tree in the garden except the tree in the middle of Eden. If they ate fruit from that tree, they would know good from evil.

*"**P**sssssssst."* One day a slithery snake talked to Eve. The snake was the most clever wild animal God had made.

The snake said, "God told you not to eat fruit from the middle tree. But that's the best fruit in the whole garden. Go ahead and eat the fruit. It will make you wise like God." So, Eve ate the fruit and then gave Adam some to eat also.

That night God came walking in the garden. He said, "Adam! Where are you?" Adam was hiding. God said, "What's wrong? Did you eat the fruit from the tree of the knowledge of good and evil?"

Adam told God that Eve gave him the fruit to eat. Then Eve said the snake had tricked her into eating it. God was upset. Adam and Eve had not obeyed Him. So, He made them leave the beautiful garden forever. It was the saddest day of all.

# Kids Life QUESTIONS

1. What was the name of the garden where Adam and Eve lived?

2. How did God feel when Adam and Eve disobeyed Him?

3. How do you feel when you disobey your parents?

## FUN & FACTS

Did you know that some snakes are so slithery that they slide right out of their skins about once a year? It's called "shedding their skins." Aren't you glad God didn't make people shed their skins?

# Rain, Rain, Rain

*Genesis 6:9–7:16*

As time went by, people in the world did bad things, just as Adam and Eve. Noah was the only good man left on earth. He loved and obeyed God.

God told Noah He was going to cover the world with water. But He promised to save Noah and his family from the flood. And He promised to save some of the world's animals, too.

God told Noah how to build a huge boat called an ark to save his family and the animals. So, Noah built the boat just as God said. It had one long window and one big door. Noah put tar inside and outside so it would not leak.

The big boat was finally finished! God told Noah to get on board. So, Mr. and Mrs. Noah, their three sons and wives got on the boat. Then God sent two of every kind of animal for Noah to put on the boat —a girl and boy of each kind.

Finally, God closed the big door. The rain began to fall. First it sprinkled. Then it poured! The water got deeper and deeper. It rained for forty days and forty nights. The whole world was covered with water. The animals and people on the big boat were safe. Everything else died.

# Kids Life QUESTIONS

1. How many people were safe on the big boat?

2. How long did it rain?

3. When it is stormy out, do you trust God to take care of you? How does He take care of you?

## FUN & FACTS

Noah's big boat was probably 150 yards long! That's as big as one and a half football fields. Ask an adult to show you a football field sometime; then you'll know how big Noah's boat was.

# Noah's Family Is Saved

*Genesis 7:17–9:29*

Back on the big boat, Noah and his family were safe and dry. The boat floated on the water for 150 days—five whole months! God had remembered His promise to save Noah.

**D**rip. Drip. Drip. Rain stopped falling from the clouds. Water stopped bubbling up from the rivers. And God made a wind blow to dry the earth. It blew and blew! Everyone on the boat was happy the flood was over.

*Kerplunk!* One day the big boat stopped floating. It stuck on a mountain top. The water was drying up. A few weeks later, the earth was all dry. So, Noah's family and all the animals came out of the boat. It was a clean new world!

God told Noah's family and the animals to have many children. Then God made a promise: He said He would never destroy the world with water again. Then He put a beautiful rainbow in the sky to help Him remember His promise. And to this very day God has kept His promise.

# Kids Life QUESTIONS

1. What was God's promise to Noah?

2. Will God always keep His promises?

3. Have you ever seen a rainbow in the sky? What colors are in God's rainbow?

## FUN & FACTS

God's rainbow always has seven wonderful colors. They are red, orange, yellow, green, blue, indigo, and violet. The next time you see a rainbow, see if you can find all seven colors. Can you find these colors in your crayons?

# God's Promise to Abram

*Genesis 15:1–17:5*

Abram was a very good man. God was pleased with him. But Abram was sad. He was an old man—100 years old!—and he did not have a son.

One night God spoke to Abram in his dream. God said He would protect Abram. He was going to give Abram a reward.

Abram told God there was nothing he wanted as a reward. He did not want more land or herds of sheep or money. He only wanted a son.

45

Then God surprised Abram! He led Abram outside. God said, "Look at the sky. There are so many stars you cannot count them. That's how many children you will have!" Then God changed Abram's name to Abraham, which means "father of many nations."

# Kids Life QUESTIONS

1. Why was Abram sad?

2. Why did God change Abram's name?

3. Can you name a promise that God has given you?

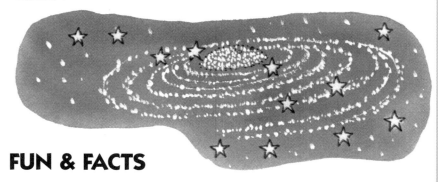

## FUN & FACTS

The Milky Way is a huge group of stars called a galaxy. There are over 200 billion stars in the Milky Way! This group of stars is so famous that a chocolate bar has even been named for it. When you go out to count the stars, ask an adult to show you the Milky Way.

# Isaac–Son and Sacrifice

*Genesis 21:1-5;  22:1-18*

About a year later, God kept His promise. Abraham's wife Sarah had a son, even though she was 90 years old! God told them to name the baby Isaac. Everyone was happy.

A few years later, God wanted to see if Abraham still loved Him more than he loved his son Isaac. So, God gave Abraham a test. He told Abraham to give Isaac to Him as a sacrifice.

Abraham took Isaac to a mountain top to worship God. They built an altar of stones and put wood on it for a fire. Then Abraham tied up Isaac and put him on top of the wood.

Abraham raised his knife to kill Isaac. But God stopped him! God knew for sure that Abraham loved Him more than Isaac. Abraham and Isaac praised God together at the altar.

# Kids Life QUESTIONS

1. How old was Sarah when she had the baby?

2. Why did God give Abraham a test?

3. Can you think of anything that is more important to you than God?

## FUN & FACTS

Altars were places where sacrifices, gifts or prayers were given to God. They were made of soil, grass, or rocks piled up in the shape of a table. Do you have a special place where you pray to God?

# Jacob Tricks Esau

*Genesis 25:29-34*

One day Isaac's younger son Jacob was making a pot of vegetable soup. His older brother Esau came home from hunting. He was very hungry.

"Mmmm, that soup smells good," thought Esau. He said to Jacob, "Let me eat some of that red soup. I am so hungry I'm weak."

Then Jacob tricked Esau. He said, "You can have some soup if you will give me your rights as the oldest son." The oldest son usually became head of the family later.

Esau was so hungry that he promised to give Jacob his rights as the oldest son. Then Jacob gave him some bread and soup. Esau was foolish to give up being head of his family for only a bowl of soup.

# Kids Life QUESTIONS

1. Was Esau or Jacob older?

2. What did Jacob want?

3. Have you ever traded something and then wished you had it back? What?

## FUN & FACTS

The oldest son in a Jewish family was called the "first-born son." He became head of the family when his father died. Jesus is called God's firstborn son. And He is head of God's family, the church.

# Joseph, A Kind Brother

*Genesis 37–45*

Jacob had twelve sons, but Joseph was his favorite. He gave Joseph a special coat to wear. This made Joseph's brothers angry. They sold Joseph to some slave traders going to Egypt.

Joseph was sold as a slave to Potiphar, an officer of the king of Egypt. Before long God helped Joseph become a very important man in Egypt.

Many years later, Joseph's brothers came to Egypt to buy food. There had been no rain in their land and no food would grow. They had to ask their brother Joseph for the food.

Joseph recognized his brothers, but they did not know who Joseph was. When they found out, they were afraid.

They had been mean to Joseph. They thought he would be mean to them, too.

But Joseph surprised them! He was kind. He sent them home to get their father and all of their belongings. He gave them land in Egypt and plenty of food to eat. God had turned evil into good.

# Kids Life QUESTIONS

1. What special gift did Joseph's father give him?

2. Are you ever jealous of your brothers or sisters?

3. How can you be kind to people who have been mean to you?

## FUN & FACTS

The King of Egypt was called Pharaoh. At first this word meant *great house*—the palace where the king lived. Later, Pharaoh was used as the title for any king who lived in the palace.

# Moses Is Born

*Exodus 2:1-10*

Joseph lived in Egypt for many years. Then he died. Years later a new king became ruler of Egypt. He did not remember the good things Joseph had done for Egypt. He treated Joseph's people, the Hebrews, like slaves. He made them work, work, work!

One Hebrew woman had a baby boy named Moses. She hid him from the mean people of Egypt for three months. Then she could not hide him anymore.

Moses' mother made a tiny basket boat and laid baby Moses inside. She put the basket in the Nile River near the edge. Moses' sister Miriam waited nearby to see what would happen.

Soon the king's daughter came to the river to take a bath. She found the basket boat and baby Moses. *Wah!* He was crying, and she felt sorry for him.

Miriam asked the princess if she would like a nurse for the baby. She said, "Yes, please." So, Miriam got Moses' own mother to take care of him.

When Moses was old enough, his mother took him to the palace. The princess adopted Moses, and he grew up in the palace. And that was right where God wanted him to be all along!

# Kids Life QUESTIONS

1. How did Moses' mother save him?

2. What did Moses' sister, Miriam, do?

3. How can you help your mother take care of your brothers or sisters?

## FUN & FACTS

In Bible times, people were often given names that told something about them. The name *Moses* means *saved from the water.* Ask an adult to help you find out what your name means.

# A Burning Bush

*Exodus 3:1–4:17*

Moses moved away from Egypt when he was older. And one day he was taking care of some sheep. *Wow! What is that?* Moses saw a bush that was on fire. But the bush did not burn up.

Moses went closer to look at the burning bush. Then God spoke to him from the fire: "Moses! Moses! Don't come any closer! Take off your shoes. You are on holy ground."

God told Moses to go back to Egypt. He wanted Moses to lead the Hebrew people out of Egypt's slavery. Moses was afraid and said, "Lord, why me? Please send someone else."

So, God sent Moses' brother Aaron with him to Egypt. And God showed Moses how to do miracles with his walking stick to make the King of Egypt believe in God. Then Moses and Aaron went to Egypt to lead the Hebrews out of slavery.

# Kids Life QUESTIONS

1. What did God want Moses to do?

2. Who did God send along with Moses?

3. When was the last time you were afraid to go somewhere you had never been before?

## FUN & FACTS

Moses' walking stick was a shepherd's staff. It was a long stick with a crook at the top. A shepherd uses his staff to guide the sheep. Sometimes he uses the crook to rescue a sheep that has fallen down a hill or into a ditch. God made Moses' walking stick change into a snake and then back to a stick again!

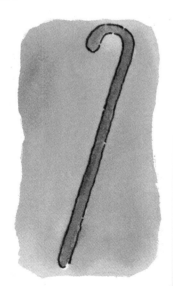

# Walking through the Sea

*Exodus 14:10-31*

Moses and Aaron led the Hebrew people out of Egypt. But the Egyptian army came after them. The army was chasing God's people across the desert!

Then the Hebrews stopped. They were in big trouble! The Red Sea was in front of them, and the army of Egypt was behind them. They were trapped! And they were scared.

Moses told the people to watch God's power at work. He held out his walking stick over the Red Sea. And God pushed the waters back on both sides with a strong wind to make a dry path for them to walk on.

God's people walked to the other side of the Red Sea. Then the army of Egypt came in their chariots. *Clompity clomp! Clompity clomp!* They followed God's people right through the sea.

God made some of the chariot wheels fall off. The Egyptians had a hard time driving their chariots. Then He told Moses to hold out his hand over the sea. And Moses did. *Crash, splash!* Suddenly, the Red Sea came crashing together and drowned the army of Egypt. God's people were safe on the other shore.

# Kids Life QUESTIONS

1. What miracle did God do for the Hebrew people?

2. Have you ever been chased by someone? Who?

3. How do you feel when someone is chasing you?

## FUN & FACTS

The Red Sea is huge! It's about 1,200 miles long and 200 miles wide in places. Sometimes it's called the Sea of Reeds because so many tall grassy reeds grow in it.

# Moses Talks to God

*Exodus 19:1–20:21*

Three months later, the Hebrew people came to the mountain called Sinai. They set up their camp in the desert near the mountain.

Climb, climb, climb. Moses went up on the mountain to talk with God. There was thick, dark smoke at the top because God came down to the mountain in a huge fire.

God loved the Hebrew people. He had chosen them for a very special job. God gave Moses ten wise teachings for the people to follow. These teachings would help them live happy lives.

God wrote the ten teachings on stone tablets with His own finger. And Moses carried them down the mountain to the people. Then Moses read the ten teachings to the people.

# The Ten Teachings of God

1. Worship God only.
2. Make God the most important part of your life.
3. Use God's name carefully.
4. Rest on God's day of worship.
5. Respect your mother and father.
6. Respect the lives of all people.
7. Keep your marriage pure.
8. Take only what belongs to you.
9. Tell the truth.
10. Be happy with what you have.

# Kids Life QUESTIONS

1. What was the name of the mountain that Moses climbed?

2. How many teachings did God give to Moses?

3. How can we live happy lives for God?

## FUN & FACTS

There were really two sets of stone tablets that had God's ten teachings on them. When Moses brought the first set down the mountain, the people were doing bad things against God. So, Moses threw the stone tablets down and broke them to show God's anger. Then God made another set of stone tablets for Moses. See Exodus 34:1.

# Rahab Helps God's Spies

*Joshua 2, 6*

After Moses died, Joshua became leader of God's people. God helped Joshua to lead His people into Canaan—the land God had promised them.

Joshua sent two spies to the city of Jericho. They went to the home of Rahab. The King of Jericho heard about the spies. He sent soldiers to capture them. But Rahab hid the spies on her roof under some plants called *flax*.

*K*nock, knock, knock! The soldiers were at Rahab's door. She told them the spies had left the city. She said, "Hurry! You might still catch them." So, the soldiers left. Rahab had saved God's spies.

Then Rahab helped the spies escape down the city wall by a rope. Rahab asked the spies to save her family when they came back to capture Jericho. They said they would.

The spies told Rahab to hang a red cord in her window so they could find her. When God's army came, Rahab and her family were rescued. She had saved God's people. So, God saved her.

# Kids Life QUESTIONS

1. How many spies did Joshua send into Jericho?

2. What did Rahab hang in the window to save her family?

3. If God's spies came to your house, where would you hide them?

## FUN & FACTS

Rahab hid the spies under *flax,* a plant that was combed and spun into thread. The thread was woven into cloth and used to make clothes and ropes. The rope Rahab used to help the spies escape may have been made of flax.

# Jericho's Walls Fall Down

*Joshua 6*

"March, march, march!" shouted Joshua to God's army. They were going to capture Jericho. God had promised Joshua that they would win the battle.

The people of Jericho were scared. They knew God was on the side of the Hebrew army. So, they locked everyone inside the city walls and waited.

At last God's army came. The first day the army marched around the walls of Jericho one time. Seven priests led the marching army.

100

The second day God's army marched around the walls again. And they did that every day for six days. The box with God's ten teachings was carried behind the priests to show that God was with them.

On the seventh day God's army marched around Jericho's walls seven times. Then the priests blew one long blast on their

horns: *"Ahhhoooooooh!"* Then God's people shouted: "Charge!" And the walls of Jericho came crashing down. God's army had won!

# Kids Life QUESTIONS

1. How many days did the Hebrews walk around the city?

2. What was carried behind the priests?

3. How can you be a real winner for God?

## FUN & FACTS

Musical instruments called *horns* today got their name from trumpets like God's priests used at Jericho. These were made from the horn of a male sheep (Joshua 6:4). The point of the horn was cut off to make a small hole to blow through and the inside of the horn was scraped out to make the musical sound.

# Deborah Leads God's Army

*Judges 4:1-16; 5*

King Jabin of Canaan had ruled over God's people, Israel, for twenty years. He was very mean to them. Israel asked God to help them.

A woman named Deborah was the leader of God's people. She sat under the Palm Tree of Deborah as a judge. There she helped the people of Israel solve problems and arguments between each other.

Deborah told Barak, "Get God's army ready to fight. God is going to help you beat King Jabin's army." Barak said, "I will only go if you go with me."

Deborah said, "I will go with you. But you will not be called the winner of the battle. God will let a woman beat King Jabin!" That day God helped Deborah, Barak, and 10,000 soldiers beat King Jabin in battle. Once again God had rescued His people.

# Kids Life QUESTIONS

1. Where did Deborah sit to help people?

2. Why did God's army go to battle?

3. Have you ever helped when two friends wanted the same toy? What did you do to solve the problem?

## FUN & FACTS

Deborah and Barak may have sung the very first "duet." A duet is when just two people sing. Judges 5 is the happy song they sang after God helped them beat Jabin's army. Ask someone to sing a duet with you. A good song to sing is "I'm in the Lord's Army."

# Samson, the Strongest Man

*Judges 13:24; 16*

Another judge of God's people was Samson. God told Samson never to cut his hair. As long as Samson obeyed, God made him strong. He was the strongest man in the whole world!

Samson fell in love with Delilah. Samson's enemies promised to give her money if she would trick him. They wanted to know why Samson was so strong. They planned to kill him.

Delilah worked hard to find out Samson's secret. She begged and cried; he would not tell her. She tied him with new ropes; he broke them. She tied him with bow strings; he got away. At last, Samson was tired of being bothered. He told Delilah his long hair was the secret to his strength.

*S*nip, snip, snip! When Samson went to sleep, Delilah had his hair cut. Samson disobeyed God. All his strength left him and Samson's enemies captured him.

W hen Samson's hair grew long again,
God made him strong enough to
destroy many of his enemies.

# Kids Life QUESTIONS

1. What made Samson strong?

2. Who was Delilah?

3. How did Samson lose his strength?

4. Do you know a special secret? Should you tell the secret?

## FUN & FACTS

Samson made a promise to belong to God in a special way. This promise was called a *Nazirite Vow.* A person making this promise was not supposed to cut his hair. He did not eat or drink anything made from grapes. God loves it when we make a special promise to Him and keep it.

# Ruth, A Loyal Woman

*Ruth 1–4*

Naomi lived far away from her home in Bethlehem. Her husband and sons had all died. Naomi was sad and lonely. She wanted to go home to God's people.

Naomi told her two sons' wives to go home to their own people. They cried and were very sad. They did not want to leave each other. But finally Orpah went home to her parents. Ruth stayed with Naomi. She was very loyal. Ruth and Naomi went to Bethlehem together.

Naomi and Ruth were very poor. Ruth worked hard picking up grain left in the field. Naomi's cousin, Boaz, owned the field. He saw how hard Ruth worked for Naomi. He told the workers to leave extra grain for her to find.

Because Boaz knew Ruth was kind to Naomi, he was kind to Ruth. Soon Ruth married Boaz, and God gave them a baby boy named Obed. Ruth and Boaz were happy parents, and Naomi was a happy grandmother!

# Kids Life QUESTIONS

1. Why was Naomi sad?

2. Who stayed with Naomi?

3. Who was Boaz?

4. Do you have a good friend whom you would do anything for?

## FUN & FACTS

The grain Ruth picked up in Boaz's field may have been barley or wheat. Did you know that wheat *prays*? When wheat is ripe, it bows its head down. Then the farmer knows it's time to gather the wheat. Maybe that is God's way of reminding the farmer to be thankful for his good crop.

# God Hears Hannah's Prayer

*I Samuel 1:1–2:11*

Hannah was very sad. She wanted a baby boy, but God had said not yet. One day at the Lord's Holy Tent, Hannah cried and prayed. She made a promise to God: If He would give her a son, she would give the boy back to serve God all of his life.

Eli the priest saw Hannah praying. He thought she was drunk. Hannah told him she was praying about her problem. Eli said, "Go in peace. May God give you what you asked for." Hannah felt better and stopped crying.

God had heard Hannah's prayer. He gave her a baby boy. She named him Samuel. Hannah was so happy!

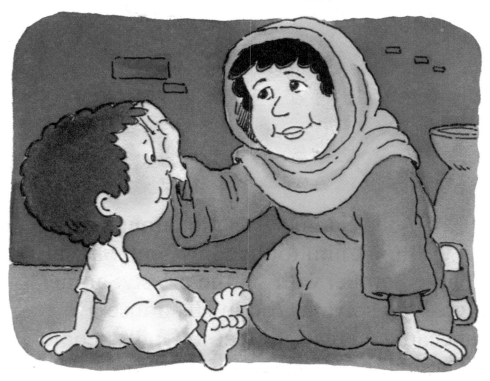

When Samuel was old enough, Hannah took him to the Holy Tent. She left little Samuel with Eli the priest. Samuel grew up serving God in His house. He became a great prophet to God's people. Hannah kept her promise to God.

# Kids Life QUESTIONS

1. Why was Hannah sad?

2. What did Eli think was wrong with Hannah?

3. What promise did Hannah make to God?

4. What is one promise that you have kept?

## FUN & FACTS

The Holy Tent was where God lived among His people. It was right in the middle of their camp. That way, they would not forget He was with them. It was also called the Meeting Tent. God met with His people there, and they worshipped Him. God's special room in the Holy Tent was called the Most Holy Place.

# Saul Becomes King

*1 Samuel 9:15–10:24*

God had always taken very good care of His people, Israel. But Israel wanted a king. They wanted to be like the other countries around them.

Samuel had become a great prophet. God said to Samuel, "Tomorrow I will send a man to you. He is from Benjamin's family. You must appoint him leader of My people."

The next day, just as God said, a man met Samuel. His name was Saul. God told Samuel, "This is the man I told you about. He will rule My people." Samuel poured olive oil on Saul's head to show he was king.

A few days later, Samuel brought all of God's people together. They stood in tribes and family groups. As the tribes walked past Samuel, God chose the tribe of Benjamin. Then He chose Matri's family group. From that family, God chose Saul.

But no one could find Saul! God said, "He's hiding behind the baggage." When they brought Saul out, he was taller than anyone else in Israel. And the people shouted, "Long live the king!"

# Kids Life QUESTIONS

1. Who was chosen to be king?

2. What did Samuel do to make Saul king?

3. How would you feel if God put you in charge of lots of people?

## FUN & FACTS

Olive oil was used in many ways in Bible times. People used it for cooking, as medicine, and for burning in lamps. Did you know that we still use olive oil for cooking and medicine today? Ask your parents if there is some olive oil in your kitchen you can see.

# David and the Giant

*I Samuel 17*

God's army was on one hill. Their enemies, the Philistines, were on the

other hill. A big valley was between them. Their enemies had a giant in their army. His name was Goliath. He was over nine feet tall!

Every day Goliath dared Israel to send a man out to fight him. But Israel's soldiers were afraid of the giant. One day a shepherd named David came to Israel's camp. He told King Saul, "I will go and fight the giant."

Saul said, "David, you are only a boy." David said, "God helped me kill a lion and a bear. He will help me kill this giant, too." David chose five stones from the brook. Then he took his sling and went to fight the giant.

*Tramp, tramp, tramp!* The giant came to attack young David. He was wearing heavy armor and carrying a huge spear. David chose a stone and put it in his sling. Around and around went the sling. *Zing!* The stone flew through the air and hit the giant in the head. Goliath fell down.

David ran to the giant and killed him. God had helped a young shepherd boy kill a giant! Then the enemies of Israel were afraid and ran away from God's people.

# Kids Life QUESTIONS

1. How tall was the giant?

2. How many stones did David pick up?

3. What made David brave enough to fight the giant?

4. Who will be with you when you need help?

## FUN & FACTS

Slings in Bible times were not like toy slings today. They were deadly weapons used by trained soldiers. The stones David used in his sling were not little pebbles either. They weighed about two pounds each. No wonder the giant Goliath fell down. David hit him right between the eyes with a two-pound rock!

# Two Good Friends

*I Samuel 18–20*

Jonathan was King Saul's son. He and David were best friends. Jonathan gave David his coat and sword as a sign of their friendship. After David killed the giant, he went to the palace to play and sing songs for the king. Saul also put David in charge of God's army. The army won many battles.

Soon the people liked David more than King Saul. This made the king angry. When he tried to kill David with a spear, David ran away. He asked Jonathan for help.

Jonathan said, "I will warn you if my father is angry with you. Tomorrow I will shoot an arrow in front of you if it's safe to come out. But if I shoot an arrow past where you're standing, you must run away." Then Jonathan went home, and David waited in the field.

The next day Jonathan came to the field. *Twang!* He shot an arrow past David. Then David knew King Saul wanted to kill him. David came out from his hiding place. He and Jonathan hugged each other. They cried because David was going away. They promised always to be friends.

# Kids Life QUESTIONS

1. Who was David's best friend?

2. Why was King Saul angry?

3. How did Jonathan warn David?

4. What is the name of your best friend?

## FUN & FACTS

When David played music for King Saul, he may have played a *lyre*. A lyre is a small harp with strings.

The book of Psalms is like a songbook. David and others wrote and sang the songs in Psalms. We still sing many songs from Psalms today. Can you sing a song about God?

# Three Mighty Men

*II Samuel 23:13-17*

David had become King of Israel. One day three of his bravest soldiers came to see him. David was hiding from his enemies in the Cave of Adullam. He was

very thirsty. He thought about the sweet water near his home. David said, "I wish someone would get me a drink from the well at Bethlehem."

David's three mighty men loved him very much. They went to get the water for David. But David did not know they went. It was a dangerous trip. The three mighty men had to fight past enemy soldiers!

146

The soldiers went all the way to Bethlehem. There they drew a jar of water from the well David loved.

The mighty men fought back through the enemy soldiers. They carried the sweet water back to King David at the cave.

King David would not drink the water they brought him. He said it would not be right for him to drink it. His mighty men had risked their lives to get it. David poured the water he wanted so badly on the ground as a gift to God. He showed his men that their gift of water was very special to him.

# Kids Life QUESTIONS

1. Who was King of Israel?

2. Why did David pour out the water instead of drinking it?

3. What very special thing do you have that you could give to God?

## FUN & FACTS

People have explored and studied caves for many years. Caves have often been used as homes by people. Hundreds of years ago, people drew pictures on the walls of caves to tell stories. Would you like to explore a cave? Maybe your family can visit a big cave sometime.

# God's Temple

*I Kings 5–6*

At last God's people were at peace. The wars were over! David's son, Solomon, was now King of Israel. God had promised David that Solomon could build His temple. It was the building where God's people could worship Him.

Solomon took seven years to build the temple. Over 183,000 men helped him to build it! They were lumbermen, wood carvers, stonecutters, and gold workers.

The lumbermen cut down special cedar trees in the country of Lebanon and they floated them down the river. Then they carried the trees across the land all the way to Jerusalem.

The stonecutters cut huge blocks of special stone out of the mountain for the temple. It took 70,000 men to carry the stones. These huge stones would become the floor of God's house.

154

The temple had three rooms. The outer courtyard was where any of God's people could worship. Only the priests could go into next room, the Holy Place. The third room was God's very special room. It was called the Most Holy Place. The High Priest went into this room only once a year.

When the temple was finished, it was wonderful! Every wall was covered with gold. Every door was covered with gold. Even the floor was covered with gold. It was the most beautiful building in the world! It was the house of God.

# Kids Life QUESTIONS

1. Which king built God's house?

2. How many men helped build the temple?

3. Where did the lumbermen get the trees to build the temple?

4. What can you do to make your church (God's house) special?

## FUN & FACTS

Lebanon means *white*. The country was named for the white snow that covers the mountains where the giant cedar trees grow. The cedars have to be strong and tough to grow in the snow. In Bible times, these giant trees were often used to build places of worship and palaces for kings.

# Wise King Solomon

*I Kings 10:1-10*

God had made King Solomon the richest and wisest man in the whole world. He was famous!

The queen of Sheba heard about Solomon's wisdom and wealth. So, she came to see if it was true. She brought many servants. She also brought camels carrying spices, jewels, and much gold.

The queen of Sheba tested King Solomon's wisdom. She asked him many hard questions. But he answered every one! She learned that he really was very wise.

Solomon showed the queen of Sheba all his riches. She was amazed! She said, "You have twice as much as anyone told me." Then she gave Solomon the spices and jewels she had brought. She also gave him 9,000 pounds of gold! Solomon really was the richest and wisest man in the world.

# Kids Life QUESTIONS

1. Who came to visit King Solomon?

2. Why did she come?

3. What gifts did the queen bring?

4. How did Solomon get to be so rich and wise? How can you become wise?

## FUN & FACTS

Solomon sent out many trading ships. They brought home gold, silver, jewels, ivory, and animals. Solomon earned about 65,000 pounds of gold a year. That is a lot of money! He was a very rich man.

# Elijah Rides a Whirlwind

*II Kings 2:1-15*

Elijah had been a great prophet for God. Now it was time for God to take Elijah to heaven. Elisha was Elijah's helper. They walked to the Jordan River side by side.

Elijah said to Elisha, "What can I do for you before I go?" Elisha said, "Give me a double share of your spirit." Elijah said, "If you see me when I go, you will have it."

*S*woosh! Suddenly a chariot and horses made of fire appeared! It came between Elijah and Elisha. Elijah dropped his coat by Elisha.

Then Elisha saw Elijah riding on a whirlwind! The whirlwind took Elijah into heaven. Elisha saw it happen, but he never saw Elijah again.

Elisha tore his own clothes to show how sad he was. Then he picked up Elijah's coat and went on his way. The Bible shows that Elisha did twice as many miracles as Elijah had done! That is because God gave Elisha a double share of Elijah's spirit.

# Kids Life QUESTIONS

1. Who was Elijah's helper?

2. What did he want from Elijah?

3. How did Elijah get to heaven?

4. How did you feel when someone special to you died or moved away?

## FUN & FACTS

Before Elijah went up into heaven, Elisha asked for a double share of Elijah's spirit. In Bible times, the oldest son in a family was the heir. He was given twice as much of his father's wealth as his brothers and sisters got. Elisha asked for a double share of Elijah's power. God gave it to him. All his life Elisha was God's spokesman to Israel.

# Elisha and the Pot of Oil

*II Kings 4:1-7*

One of God's prophets died. His wife came to Elisha and said, "My husband owed a man some money. I cannot pay him. So, he is coming to take my two sons. He will make them his slaves!"

Elisha said, "What can I do to help you? What do you have in your house?"

The woman said, "I only have one pot of oil."

"Get as many empty jars as you can from your neighbors," Elisha said. "Get lots of them! Fill the jars full of oil from your pot."

The woman's sons brought many jars to her. God helped her fill all the jars. She said, "Bring me another jar."

"There are no more jars," her son said. Then the oil stopped flowing.

The woman told Elisha. He said, "Go and sell the jars of oil. Pay the man what your husband owed him. Then you and your sons can live on the rest of the money." And that is what she did. God had saved her sons from being slaves.

# Kids Life QUESTIONS

1. How many pots of oil did the woman have at first?

2. How could she fill lots of jars from only one pot?

3. How did God help the woman?

4. How could God help you with one of your problems?

## FUN & FACTS

Elisha's name means *God is salvation.* He spoke to Israel for God. Elisha often showed the people how God had saved them. In this story, God used Elisha to save the woman and her two sons. Elisha really did live up to his name!

# Joash, the Boy King

*II Kings 11:21–2:16*

God's people had split into two groups. One group was called Israel. The other group was called Judah. Joash was made king of Judah. He was only seven years old! Joash did what the Lord said was right. He was a good king.

When he was older, God's temple needed to be repaired. King Joash told the priests to repair it. He said to use the money God's people brought to the temple.

Many years later the temple was still not repaired. So, workers were hired to repair it. A special box was put in the temple. God's people brought money and put it in the box. The money was used to pay the carpenters, stonecutters, and builders.

At last God's temple was repaired. King Joash had done a very good thing. Joash was king of Judah for forty years because he did what God said was right.

# Kids Life QUESTIONS

1. What are the names of the two groups of God's people?

2. How old was Joash when he became king of Judah?

3. Do you think you would make a good king or queen?

4. What is one thing that you do to please the Lord?

## FUN & FACTS

People in Bible times were called by different names. One name they called God's people was *Jew*. This name was like a nickname. It was short for Judah. God's people soon became known as the Jewish nation.

# Brave Queen Esther

*Esther 2–5*

Esther was a beautiful woman. She was one of God's people, the Jews. King Xerxes of Persia chose Esther to become his queen. He loved her very much.

Haman was the king's most important helper. He hated Jews. One day Haman tricked King Xerxes into making a law to kill the Jews. He sealed it with the king's royal seal. But Haman did not know that Esther was a Jew.

Esther found out about Haman's trick. Her people were all going to be killed. She had to stop Haman! But she could only go to the king if he sent for her. Otherwise he might have her killed. That was the law.

Esther had to go before the king. She prayed to God for help. She did not eat for three days. Then she dressed in her best robe and crown and waited outside the king's throne room. When he saw her, he asked her to come in. He said, "You can have anything you want, even half of my kingdom."

Esther told the king about Haman's trick. She told him about the evil plan to kill her people. The king became very angry. He ordered his soldiers to hang Haman. Brave Queen Esther had trusted God. She had saved God's people!

# Kids Life QUESTIONS

1. Who became the new queen of Persia?

2. What did the king offer to give Esther?

3. How many days did Esther not eat any food?

4. What is a prayer that you can say when you have something hard to do?

## FUN & FACTS

In Bible times, people used hot wax to seal important papers. While the wax was hot, they pressed a *seal* into it. The seal showed who the paper was from. As it cooled, the wax got hard. To open the paper, the wax seal had to be broken. Seals were worn as rings or on cords around people's necks. Some people still use wax and seals today.

# The Shepherd's Song

*Psalm 23*

This is one of the songs that David wrote.
He may have sung this song to King Saul.

The Lord is like a shepherd, and I am His sheep. He gives me everything I need. He gives me places to rest, like sheep rest in a pretty green pasture.

I am never thirsty when the Lord is near. He shows me where sweet water is. I drink and feel strong again.

The Lord leads me down the right paths. Even if the path goes through a dark valley, I am not afraid. He is always there to protect and guide me.

The Lord gives me plenty to eat, even when my enemies are watching. He makes me rich. He gives me more than I can even hold! I know that the Lord's goodness and love will be with me all my life. And I will live with Him forever.

# Kids Life QUESTIONS

1. Why are the sheep not afraid in the dark valley?

2. What makes the sheep feel strong again?

3. How long will the sheep live with the shepherd?

4. How long can you live with God?

## FUN & FACTS

Look at how God made sheep and shepherds need each other! The sheep need the shepherd to protect them, feed them, and help them find water. And the shepherd needs the sheep's wool to make himself a warm coat for winter. That is why they take care of each other. Isn't God wise?

# Three Men in a Fire

*Daniel 3:1-30*

God's people had been taken as slaves to Babylon. The king of Babylon did not know God. He built a huge gold statue for the people to worship. It was a false god. When the music played, all the people were told to bow down to the statue. If they did not bow down, they would be thrown into a huge fire!

*B**oom, boom! Toot, toot!* The music played. All the people bowed down to the statue except three Jews. Shadrach, Meshach, and Abednego knew they should worship only God in heaven. They did not bow down to the statue.

The king of Babylon became very angry. He said, "You three men must worship my gold statue. If you don't, I will throw you into the fire. Then no god can save you." But Shadrach, Meshach, and Abednego would not bow down to the statue.

The huge fire crackled in the furnace. It was seven times hotter than usual. Soldiers tied up the three men and threw them into the fire. But when the king looked, he could see four men in the fire. They were up walking around. The fire did not hurt them!

The king of Babylon called the three men out of the fire. Then he praised God! He said, "Your God has sent an angel to save you from the fire. No other god can save His people like this." And he was right!

# Kids Life QUESTIONS

1. What were the three boys' names in this story?

2. How did the people worship the statue?

3. Why did the three boys in the fire not burn up?

4. What is one way you can worship God?

## FUN & FACTS

The statue built by the king of Babylon was huge. It was ninety feet tall and nine feet wide! The whole statue was covered with pure gold. Even so, this god was nothing compared to the real God in heaven. God is bigger than the universe, and He owns the whole world.

# Daniel and the Lions

*Daniel 6:1-28*

Daniel was one of God's people in Babylon. He was an important person under King Darius. The king liked Daniel very much. Daniel was honest and worked hard.

Darius was planning to put Daniel in charge of his whole kingdom. This made the king's other leaders angry. They made a plan to get rid of Daniel. The leaders asked the king to make a law that no one could pray to anyone except King Darius. If they did, they would be thrown to the lions.

Daniel heard about the new law. But he prayed to God three times a day anyway. The evil men reported him to the king. The king was very sad. He did not want to hurt Daniel, but the law could not be changed. He had Daniel put into the lions' den. He said, "May the God you serve save you!"

The king could not sleep all night. He was worried about Daniel. The next morning he hurried to the lions' den. Daniel was alive! God had closed the lions' mouths, and they did not hurt him.

King Darius had the other evil leaders put into the lions' den. Then he passed a new law. The law said everyone in his kingdom should respect and fear the God of Daniel. It said, "Daniel's God is the living God. He lives forever."

# Kids Life QUESTIONS

1. Why were the king's other leaders angry with Daniel?

2. How many times did Daniel pray every day?

3. Why didn't the lions eat Daniel?

4. Can you think of a time when God protected you from danger?

## FUN & FACTS

Did you know that lions are lazy? Most lions sleep about fifteen hours a day. But when they do get up, they can run as fast as forty miles per hour! Lions live in certain areas. They mark off their areas with their roars. With a good wind, a lion's roar can be heard up to five miles away!

# Jonah Runs from God

*Jonah 1–4*

Jonah was a prophet. He was one of God's spokesmen. God said to Jonah, "Go preach against the people of the city of Nineveh. They have done bad things."

Jonah did not want to go to Nineveh. So, he ran away from God. He got on a boat and sailed away. But soon a big storm came. *Splash! Slosh!* Water was coming into the boat. The sailors were afraid. They thought the boat was going to sink!

Jonah said, "This storm is all my fault. I ran away from God. You must throw me into the sea. Then the storm will stop." The sailors did not want to hurt Jonah. But there was no other way to save the boat.

At last the sailors threw Jonah into the sea. God sent a big fish to swallow Jonah. He was inside the fish for three whole days. Slick and slimy seaweed was round his head. It was awful!

Jonah was sorry he had run from God. He prayed for God to forgive him and save him. Then God made the big fish spit Jonah out on the beach. Jonah got up and went to Nineveh to preach as God had told him to do.

# Kids Life QUESTIONS

1. What did God tell Jonah to do?

2. Why did Jonah run away?

3. What happened to Jonah when the sailors threw him off the boat?

4. What is one thing that you do to obey God?

## FUN & FACTS

Nineveh was one of the oldest and most important cities in the world. It was a huge city with lots of people. The city was so big that it took three days just to walk across it! God had given Jonah a big job to do.

# Mary and the Angel

*Luke 1:26-38*

Mary was a Jewish girl. She was pure and good. One day an angel named Gabriel came to see Mary. Mary was afraid. Gabriel said, "Do not be afraid, Mary. God has chosen you for a special job!"

The angel told Mary she was going to have a baby boy. He would be the most important baby ever born. He would be the Son of God!

The angel said, "Name the baby *Jesus*.
He will save people from the wrong
things they do."

Mary said, "I am the servant of the Lord.
Let this happen as you say." Then the angel
went away.

# Kids Life QUESTIONS

1. What was the Jewish girl's name?

2. Who came to visit Mary?

3. What would the baby's name be?

4. When the baby grew up, what would He do to help people?

## FUN & FACTS

The Bible books Matthew, Mark, Luke, and John are called the *Gospels.* Gospel means *good news.* These books tell the same story. They tell how Jesus was born, lived, died, and came back to life to save us. Now, that is good news!

# Jesus Is Born

*Luke 2:1-7*

At this time, God's people were being ruled by the Romans. The Roman ruler, Augustus Caesar, made a new law. He said all people must sign their names in a register. They had to sign the register in their own home towns.

Mary and Joseph went to Bethlehem to sign their names in the register. It was a long and tiring trip for Mary. She was going to have her baby soon.

In Bethlehem, Mary and Joseph stopped at an inn. (An inn is like a hotel.) But the inn was full. There were no rooms left for Mary and Joseph. So they spent the night in a stable where animals live.

That very night the baby was born! Mary wrapped Him in cloth. She used the animals' feeding box as a bed for the baby. Mary and Joseph named the baby *Jesus* just as God had told them to do. It was a wonderful night. The Son of God had been born!

# Kids Life QUESTIONS

1. Who was Joseph?

2. What did God tell Mary and Joseph to call the baby?

3. Where did baby Jesus sleep?

4. Who was Jesus?

## FUN & FACTS

Jesus was also called *Immanuel,* which means *God is with us.* Jesus was really God Himself growing up as a man. Many people did not know that Jesus was really God because He was man as well. God did not want people to be afraid of Him. He wanted people to know and love Him as they loved each other.

# Shepherds Visit Baby Jesus

*Luke 2:8-20*

The night Jesus was born some shepherds got a surprise. They were taking care of their sheep in a nearby field. Suddenly, an angel of the Lord appeared and the shepherds were very afraid.

The angel said, "Do not be afraid. I am bringing you good news. Everybody will be happy about it. Today a Savior was born in Bethlehem. He is Christ the Lord! You will find the baby wrapped in cloth and lying in a feeding box. The baby's name is Jesus."

Then a large group of angels from heaven began praising God. They said, "Give glory to God in heaven! And on earth let there be peace to the people who please God." Then the angels disappeared.

The shepherds said to each other, "Let's go to Bethlehem and see what has happened." And off they went to Bethlehem.

Soon the shepherds found baby Jesus. He was lying in the feeding box just as the angel had said. The shepherds told the people what the angel said about Jesus. Everyone was amazed!

Then the shepherds went back to their sheep. They were praising God and thanking Him for everything they had seen and heard. It was just as the angel had said. God's Son had been born!

# Kids Life QUESTIONS

1. What was the surprise the shepherds got?

2. What did the angel tell them had happened?

3. Why did the shepherds praise and thank God?

4. What is one way that we can praise God at Christmastime?

## FUN & FACTS

Did you know that sheep are not very clever? They often get lost and can't find their way home. They have to have help to find fresh water and green grass. Sometimes they fall into a ditch and must be helped out. That is why they need a shepherd so badly. God says people are sometimes like sheep. We need Jesus, the Good Shepherd, to lead us and keep us safe.

# Wise Men Bring Gifts

*Matthew 2:1-12*

When Jesus was born, God put a bright new star in the sky. The star showed people that God's Son had been born. He was to be King of the world.

Some wise men saw the new star. They lived far away in the east. The wise men followed the new star all the way to Jerusalem. They wanted to see the baby King. The trip took them a long time.

At this time Herod was king. The wise men went to Herod to ask for help: "Where is the baby who was born to be the king of the Jews? We saw His star in the east. We have come to worship Him."

When Herod heard there was a new king of the Jews, he got worried. He thought this new king might take his place. He called all his priests and teachers to help him. They said, "The Christ is to be born in Bethlehem."

Then Herod had a meeting with the wise men. He said, "Go to Bethlehem and find the child. When you find Him, come and tell me. I want to worship Him, too." But when they left, the wise men followed the new star again.

The star led the wise men to the house where Jesus was. They were so happy! They gave Jesus special gifts of myrrh and frankincense. They also gave Him gold. They bowed down and worshipped Jesus.

When the wise men left, God spoke to them in a dream. He told them not to go back to Herod. Herod wanted to kill Jesus. The wise men went home to their own country by a different way.

# Kids Life QUESTIONS

1. How did the wise men know that Jesus had been born?

2. How did the wise men find baby Jesus?

3. What gifts did the wise men bring to Jesus?

4. What gift could you give to Jesus?

## FUN & FACTS

The wise men gave Jesus myrrh and frankincense. Myrrh was a sweet-smelling liquid. It came from certain trees and shrubs. It was used as a perfume and to stop pain. Frankincense was a perfume, too. It cost lots of money. It comes from inside the terebinth tree that grows in Arabia.

# The Boy Jesus

*Luke 2:40-52*

Jesus began to grow up. He became stronger and wiser. God was with Him all the time.

Every year Jesus' parents went to Jerusalem. They went to enjoy a special feast called Passover. When Jesus was twelve years old, they went to the feast. They travelled with their friends and family.

When the feast days were over, Jesus' parents started home. The boy Jesus was still in Jerusalem. But His parents did not know it. They thought He was with their family or friends.

They travelled one whole day. Then Jesus' parents began to look for Him. But He was not there! They hurried back to Jerusalem to look for Him. They looked and looked for three whole days.

At last they found Jesus. He was in the temple talking to the teachers of God's Word. He was listening to them and asking questions. Everyone was amazed at how wise He was to be so young. Even His parents were amazed.

Jesus' mother asked, "Son, why did You do this to us? Your father and I were very worried about You. We have been looking for You."

But Jesus said, "Why did you have to look for Me? You should have known I would be in God's house."

Then Jesus went back home with His parents. He obeyed them. He kept on growing up. People liked Jesus, and He pleased God.

# Kids Life QUESTIONS

1. How old was Jesus in this story?

2. Where did Jesus' parents find Him in Jerusalem?

3. What was Jesus doing when His parents found Him?

4. How can you study God's Word?

## FUN & FACTS

Passover is the most important holy day that God gave to His people. It helps them remember when God decided to *pass over* their houses in Egypt. He saved their children from death. The Jews have a Passover supper every year in the spring. This is to honor God who saved their ancestors from slavery in Egypt.

# John Baptizes Jesus

*Matthew 3:13-17*

Many years later John the Baptist was preaching in the desert. Jesus came to see John at the Jordan River.

Jesus wanted John to baptize Him. But John tried to stop Jesus. He said, "Why do You come to me to be baptized? I should be baptized by You!"

Jesus said, "We need to do everything the right way. So, you baptize Me for now."

John and Jesus went out into the Jordan River. John baptized Jesus. Then Jesus walked up out of the river.

At that moment heaven opened! God's Spirit came down on Jesus, looking like a dove. A voice spoke, "This is My Son, and I love Him. I am very pleased with Him." It was the voice of God!

244

# Kids Life QUESTIONS

1. What was John the Baptist doing in the desert?

2. Why did Jesus go to see John?

3. Why was God pleased with Jesus?

4. What are some ways that you can please God?

## FUN & FACTS

John the Baptist lived in the desert and wore clothes made of camel's hair. He ate natural foods like locusts and wild honey. John and Jesus were members of the same family group—they were cousins. John's job was to get people ready for Jesus to come. He told people to turn away from doing bad things.

# Jesus Teaches the People

*Matthew 5–7*

When Jesus was about thirty years old, He started preaching. Big crowds of people followed Him to listen to Him speak. One day Jesus went up on the side of a mountain to teach the people about God.

That day Jesus told the people they were like lights. He said, "You are the light that gives light to the world. Don't hide your light under a bowl! Live so that people can see the good things you do. Live so they will praise God."

Jesus also said that people should not be angry with each other. He said we should make peace with others. Then we can be at peace with God, too.

Another thing Jesus taught the people was this: love other people. He said, "Don't just love your friends. Love your enemies, too. Love them the same way you love yourself." Then you will be like God in heaven.

# Kids Life QUESTIONS

1. What did Jesus say about getting angry?

2. How did Jesus want us to treat our enemies?

3. How can you show love to other people?

## FUN & FACTS

One part of Jesus' sermon on the mountain is called the Beatitudes. That word means *blessed* or *happy*. Jesus told the people eight ways to be happy. The Beatitudes are in Matthew 5:3-10. Why not read them right now with someone?

# Jesus' First Miracle

*John 2:1-12*

J esus and His followers went to a wedding. It was in the city of Cana in the area called Galilee. Jesus' mother was there, too.

The wedding guests drank all the wine. Jesus' mother said to Him, "They have no more wine."

"Why are you telling Me?" Jesus said. It's not time for Me to do miracles yet."

But His mother said to the servants, "Do what He says to do."

Jesus saw six big, stone water jars nearby. Each jar held about 30 gallons of water. Jesus told the servants to fill the jars with water. So they filled them to the top.

Jesus said to the servants, "Take some water out of one of the jars. Give it to the master of the wedding." *Mmmmm!* When he tasted it, the water had become wine! The master did not know where the servants got the wine.

The master of the wedding talked to the groom. He said, "People always serve the best wine first. But you have saved the best wine until now." This was Jesus' first miracle. When His followers saw what happened, they believed in Him.

# Kids Life QUESTIONS

1. Where did Jesus and His followers go?

2. What did Jesus' mother ask Him to do?

3. Why did Jesus' followers believe He was God's Son?

4. Can you name something that Jesus has done for you?

## FUN & FACTS

Wine is made from the juice of grapes. In Jesus' time the grapes were put in a big pit called a *winepress.* People stepped on the grapes with their bare feet to press the juice out of them. The juice drained into a barrel and was used to make wine.

# Jesus Chooses Twelve Helpers

*Mark 3:13-19*

Jesus chose twelve men to be His special helpers. They are called *apostles*. He wanted these twelve men to stay close to Him.

These twelve men had special jobs to do to help Jesus. He wanted to send them to different cities and countries. There they would tell other people the Good News about God.

Jesus gave the apostles special powers that other men did not have. They could force evil demons to come out of people. They could do wonderful things to show that God was with them.

ere are the men Jesus chose as His special helpers: Peter, Andrew, James, John, Matthew, Simon, James the son of Alphaeus, Philip, Bartholomew, Thomas, Thaddaeus, and Judas Iscariot.

# Kids Life QUESTIONS

1. Where did the apostles get their powers?

2. What special job did Jesus give them to do?

3. How many of the twelve apostles can you name?

4. How can you be a special helper for God?

## FUN & FACTS

Later, others were called apostles. One was Matthias, who was a tax collector. He took Judas Iscariot's place after Judas gave Jesus to His enemies. Another apostle was Paul, whom Jesus chose to preach the Good News about Him.

# A Little Boy's Lunch

*John 6:1-15*

One day a large crowd of people came to hear Jesus preach. Jesus said to Philip, "Where can we buy bread for all these people to eat?"

Philip said, "We would have to work a month to do that!"

Andrew said, "Here is a boy who has his lunch with him. He has five small loaves of bread and two little fish. But that is not enough for all these people."

Jesus said, "Ask the people to sit down." It was a place with lots of grass. There were five thousand men who sat down!

Jesus thanked God for the bread and gave it to the people. He did the same thing with the fish. He gave them as much as they wanted to eat. Everyone had enough to eat.

All the people finished eating. Jesus said to His helpers, "Pick up the food that is left. Don't waste anything." There were twelve baskets of bread and fish pieces left.

The people had seen Jesus feed
thousands of people with a little boy's
lunch. It was a miracle! That is how they
knew Jesus was from God.

# Kids Life QUESTIONS

1. How many people came to hear Jesus preach?

2. Where did Jesus get the five loaves of bread and two fish?

3. What do you have that Jesus can use to help other people?

## FUN & FACTS

The word *miracle* means *wonderful thing.* Miracles are wonderful things that can only be done with God's help. They are special signs to show God's power. In the Old Testament, God used miracles to rescue His people. In the New Testament, Jesus used miracles to prove that He was God's Son.

# Jesus Walks on the Lake

*Matthew 14:22-33*

Jesus told His followers to get into their boat. He told them to go ahead of Him across the lake. Jesus stayed there to say goodbye to the people. Then He went up on a hill alone to pray.

When Jesus finished praying, it was
very late. It was between three and
six o'clock in the morning. The boat was
having trouble far out on the lake. The
winds and waves were hitting against it.

Jesus walked on the water towards the boat. His followers saw Him coming, but they did not know it was Jesus. They thought He was a ghost! They were afraid.

Jesus said to them, "Be brave. Don't be afraid. It is Me."

Peter said, "Lord, if it really is You, let me walk to You on the water."

"Come," Jesus said.

Peter climbed out of the boat and walked to Jesus on the water! Then he thought about the wind and waves. He became afraid, and sank in the water.

Peter thought he was going to drown. He shouted to Jesus, "Lord, save me!"

Jesus saved Peter. He said, "Why did you doubt? Your faith is small." Jesus and Peter got into the boat.

Then His followers worshipped Jesus. They said, "You really are the Son of God!"

# Kids Life QUESTIONS

1. What did Jesus do in this story?

2. Who did Jesus' followers think He was when they saw Him walking on the lake?

3. Why do you think Peter started to sink?

4. When you are afraid, what is one thing that you could do?

## FUN & FACTS

Certain kinds of insects can walk on water like Jesus and Peter did. They are called *water striders.* Their very long legs help them to skate (or stride) along the top of the water. But they don't sink down into the water like Peter did. God is so wonderful! He can make bugs walk on water!

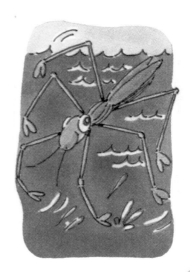

# A Blind Man Can See

*John 9:1-12*

Jesus and His followers were walking along and saw a blind man. The man had been blind since he was born. Jesus said the man was blind so that God could show how powerful He is.

Jesus spit on the ground and made some mud. He put the mud on the blind man's eyes. He told the blind man, "Go and wash in the Pool of Siloam."

The blind man went to the pool and washed his eyes. Then he could see! God's power had healed him. The people who saw him were surprised. They argued about whether it really was the blind man or not. But the blind man said, "Yes, I am the man who was born blind."

The people asked, "What happened? How did you get your sight?" The man told them what Jesus had done. They said, "Where is this man Jesus?"

"I don't know," the man born blind said. Jesus was no longer there.

# Kids Life QUESTIONS

1. Why did Jesus spit on the ground to make mud?

2. Where did Jesus tell the blind man to go and wash?

3. What can you do to help a blind person?

## FUN & FACTS

The Pool of Siloam was underground at first. The water in the pool came through a tunnel from a spring outside the city walls. The tunnel was 1,750 feet long and it was cut through solid rock! The Pool of Siloam was very important. Most people in Jerusalem got their water from this source.

# A Good Man Stops to Help

*Luke 10:25-37*

Jesus told this story about being a good neighbor to a teacher of God's law. A man was going down the road from Jerusalem to Jericho. Some robbers attacked him. They tore off his clothes, and they beat him. Then they left him lying by the road. He was almost dead.

A Jewish priest came down the road. He saw the hurt man in the ditch. But he did not stop to help. He walked by on the other side of the road.

Next, a priest's helper came along the road. He went over and looked at the hurt man. Then he walked by on the other side of the road, too. He did not stop to help.

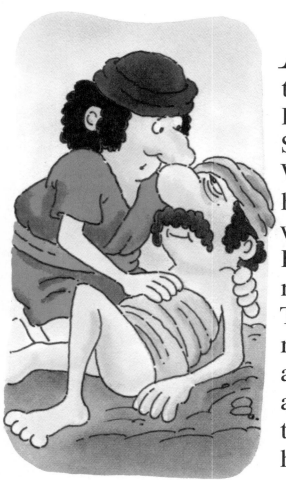

At last, along came one of the man's enemies. He was a Samaritan man. When he saw the hurt man, he felt very sorry for him. He bandaged the man's wound. Then he put the man on his donkey and took him to an inn. There he took care of the hurt man.

The next day, the Samaritan man gave two coins to the innkeeper. He said, "Take care of this man. If you spend more money on him than this, I will pay you when I come back."

When the story was finished, Jesus asked the teacher of the law a question, "Which one of these three men was a good neighbor to the hurt man?"

The teacher said, "The one who stopped to help him."

Jesus said, "Go and be a good neighbor, too."

# Kid's Life QUESTIONS

1. How many people passed by the hurt man?

2. Who *should* have helped the hurt man?

3. Who really *did* help the hurt man?

4. What is one way that you could be a good neighbor?

## FUN & FACTS

The road from Jerusalem down to Jericho was very dangerous. It was seventeen miles long and downhill all the way. The road went through rocky, desert country. It had lots of places for robbers to hide and attack people coming by. That is why Jesus used this road in His story.

# A Lost Son Is Found

*Luke 15:11-24*

Jesus told the Pharisees and teachers a story about a man who had two sons. The younger son took his share of his father's wealth and left home.

The young son went far away to another country. There he spent all his money. He wasted it on foolish things.

There was no rain in that country. So, there was not enough food for people to eat. The young man was very hungry.

He tried to get a job. The only job he could get was feeding pigs. He was so hungry, he wanted to eat what the pigs were eating.

Then the young man thought, "I have been very foolish. Even my father's servants have enough food to eat. But I am here starving. I will go home and ask my father to take me back as a servant." So he went to his father's house.

While the son was still a long way off, his father saw him coming. He felt sorry for his son. He ran to him and hugged and kissed him. Then he gave a big party. He was so happy his lost son had been found.

# Kids Life QUESTIONS

1. What happened to the young son's money?

2. What finally made the son want to go back home?

3. Why did the father give a big party?

4. How does God show His love for us?

## FUN & FACTS

In Jesus' time there were two groups of religious leaders—the *Pharisees* and *Sadducees*. Here is how to remember them. The Pharisees believed a person like Jesus could die and be raised back to life. This belief is true and very "fair, you see." The Sadducees did not believe a person could be raised back to life. This is wrong and very "sad, you see."

# A Poor Woman's Gift

*Mark 12:41-44*

Jesus was sitting near the money box in the temple. He was watching the people put in their gifts for God.

First came the rich people. *Jingle, jingle, jingle!* They put in lots of money.

N ext came a poor woman who had no husband. *Plink, plink.* She gave two very small copper coins. These coins were not even worth a penny.

Jesus called His followers over to Him. He said, "This poor widow gave only two small coins. But she really gave more than all those rich people did. Rich people have lots of money. They just give what they don't need. This poor woman gave everything she had. And she needed that money to help her live."

# Kids Life QUESTIONS

1. How much money did the poor woman give?

2. Which gift did Jesus think was best?

3. Why did Jesus say the poor woman's gift was best?

4. What gift would you like to give God?

## FUN & FACTS

The coins that the poor woman put in the money box in the temple were called *mites*. The real name for them was *Mite of Coponius*. You would need eight of them just to make a penny!

# The Last Supper

*Luke 22:7-20; I Corinthians 11:23-26*

Every year God's people ate the Passover meal. The meal helped them remember how God had saved them from slavery in Egypt. Jesus had asked Peter and John to get the Passover meal ready. They would eat it together in an upstairs room.

When the meal was ready, Jesus and His helpers sat down. Jesus said, "I wanted to eat this Passover meal with you before I die. The next time we eat it, we will be in the kingdom of God. Then it will have even more meaning."

Jesus took some bread. He thanked God for it and gave it to His helpers. He said, "This bread will remind you of My body. Think of Me when you eat it."

Then Jesus took a cup of wine. He gave thanks to God for it. He said, "This cup shows the new agreement from God to His people. The new agreement will begin when I die. This wine will remind you of My blood. When you drink the wine, do it to remember Me." After the supper, they sang a song and left.

Now, every time we eat the bread and
drink the wine, we remember Jesus.
And we show other people about His death.
We will keep on doing this until Jesus
comes again.

# Kids Life QUESTIONS

1. What was the Passover meal supposed to remind God's people of?

2. What was the Passover meal?

3. Where did Jesus and His helpers eat the Passover meal?

4. Jesus said the bread and wine should remind us of something. What?

## FUN & FACTS

During the Passover meal each Jewish family sang songs. These songs praised God and thanked Him for saving them from slavery. You can read the words to the songs they sang: Psalms 113, 114, 115, 116, 117, 118, and 136. Maybe you can make up a tune to one of these songs and sing it.

# Soldiers Arrest Jesus

*Mark 14:32-50*

After the Last Supper, Jesus and His helpers went to the Mount of Olives. This was a mountain where many olive trees grew. Jesus went off by Himself and prayed three diffferent times. His helpers fell asleep.

Jesus came back and said, "Get up! We must go. Here comes the man who will give Me to My enemies." *Tromp, tromp, tromp*! At that moment Judas Iscariot brought a group of soldiers and other people to Jesus. Judas had been one of Jesus' helpers.

These people were sent by the leading priests, teachers of God's law, and the older Jewish leaders. They all had swords and clubs! Judas had told the soldiers to watch for his signal. He would kiss the man who was Jesus.

Judas came up to Jesus and said, "Teacher!" He kissed Jesus. Then the men grabbed Jesus and arrested Him.

Jesus said, "These things have happened to make the Scriptures come true." Then all of Jesus' helpers left Him and ran away.

# Kids Life QUESTIONS

1. Who gave Jesus to His enemies?

2. Why did Judas kiss Jesus?

3. Why do you think Jesus' helpers ran away?

4. Did you ever run away from something you were afraid of? Why?

## FUN & FACTS

Judas was an evil man. He had taken care of the money for Jesus and His helpers. But he had stolen some of it for himself. In this part of the story, he sells Jesus to His enemies for 30 silver coins. For that little bit of money, Judas sold the Son of God.

# Jesus Dies

*Matthew 27:32-61; Mark 15:16-47*

Jesus was put on trial. Because people lied about Him to the judge, Jesus was found guilty. They said He had to die on a cross.

On Friday, the soldiers beat Jesus. He was very weak. He could not carry the heavy wooden cross to the place where they would crucify Him. The soldiers made a man named Simon carry the cross for Jesus.

The soldiers led Jesus to a place called Golgotha. It was a hill outside of Jerusalem. There they nailed Jesus to the cross. Then the soldiers gambled for Jesus' clothes. It was nine o'clock in the morning.

A sign was nailed to Jesus' cross. It said, "The King of the Jews." Two robbers were nailed to crosses, too. People walked by and said ugly things to Jesus. "Save Yourself! Come down from the cross, if You are the Son of God!"

At noon, the whole country became dark. The darkness lasted for three hours. At three o'clock, Jesus died for the sins of the world.

When Jesus died, the huge curtain in the temple split into two pieces. It ripped from top to bottom! The earth shook, and rocks broke apart! Graves opened, and dead people came back to life. The soldiers guarding Jesus said, "He really was the Son of God!"

On Friday evening, Jesus was buried. A man named Joseph buried Him in his own new tomb. A huge stone was put in front of the opening. Jesus was dead, and His followers were very sad.

# Kids Life QUESTIONS

1. Who made the earth get dark when Jesus was dying?

2. Who buried Jesus?

3. On what day of the week did Jesus die?

4. How do you feel when you think about Jesus dying on the cross?

## FUN & FACTS

The curtain that tore in two when Jesus died was very special. It was woven of blue, purple, and scarlet yarn and finely twisted linen cloth. On it were sewn wonderful pictures of cherubim (angels). The curtain was fifteen feet high and about four inches thick! So, it did not tear by itself—God had to do it.

# Jesus Lives Again

*Matthew 28:1-10*

Early Sunday morning two women went to look at Jesus' grave. They were Mary Magdalene and another woman named Mary.

At that time there was a strong earthquake! An angel of the Lord came down from heaven. *Rumble, rumble.* He rolled the stone away from Jesus' tomb. He was shining as bright as a flash of lightning. His clothes were as white as new snow.

The soldiers guarding the tomb were very frightened of the angel. They shook with fear. Then they became as still as dead men.

The angel said to the two women, "Don't be afraid. I know that you are looking for Jesus who died. He is not here. He has come back to life! It's just as He said it would be. Go quickly and tell His followers that He is alive!"

The women were afraid, but they were so happy! They ran to tell Jesus' followers what had happened. As they were going, Jesus met them. They bowed down, held on to Jesus' feet, and worshipped Him. Jesus said, "Don't be afraid. Go and tell My helpers to go to Galilee. They will see Me there."

The two women ran to tell Jesus' helpers that He was alive. The eleven helpers went to Galilee. They went to the mountain where Jesus told them to go. On the mountain they saw Jesus and worshipped Him. Jesus was alive again!

# Kids Life QUESTIONS

1. Who were the two women at Jesus' tomb on Sunday morning?

2. What did the angel say?

3. Why were the two Marys so happy?

4. How can Jesus help us because He's alive today?

## FUN & FACTS

The word *angel* is a Greek word that means *messenger*. Angels are beings from heaven. They can sometimes look like people. God used angels to help His people and to announce important events. Angels announced the birth of Jesus to the shepherds. Now, they were announcing that Jesus had risen from the dead!

# Jesus Goes Back to Heaven

*Acts 1:6-12*

Jesus and His helpers were all together. They were on the Mount of Olives just outside of Jerusalem. Jesus knew it was time for Him to go back to heaven. He said, "The Holy Spirit will come to you. Then you will receive special power."

Jesus told His helpers what He wanted them to do. He said, "You will tell the Good News about Me in Jerusalem and all of the country of Judea. After that you will tell the whole region of Samaria. Then you will tell every part of the world."

After He said this, Jesus was lifted up in the air! His helpers were all watching. A cloud hid Him, and they could not see Him. As He was going, they were looking into the sky.

$S$uddenly, two men in bright white clothes were standing beside them. They said, "Why are you looking into the sky? You saw Jesus go into heaven. Don't worry. He will come back someday the same way He left." The helpers then went back to Jerusalem.

# Kids Life QUESTIONS

1. Where did Jesus go?

2. What did He want His helpers to do after He was gone?

3. What do you know about Jesus that you could share with a friend?

4. God's Spirit can help you tell others about Him. What else can God's Spirit help you do?

## FUN & FACTS

Jesus went to heaven in a cloud. There are seven different kinds of clouds. God uses them to make it rain on the flowers and crops. Watching clouds is fun. Sometimes you can see interesting shapes in the clouds. You might also see Jesus coming back! The Bible says He will come back the same way He left—in a cloud.

# The Holy Spirit Comes

*Acts 2*

When Jesus went back to heaven, He made a promise to His helpers. He promised them that the Holy Spirit would come to help them. About fifty days later, on the Day of Pentecost, Jesus' helpers were all together.

Suddenly they heard a loud noise. It sounded like a rushing wind blowing from heaven. The sound filled the whole house where they were sitting.

Next Jesus' followers saw something strange. They saw what looked like tongues of fire. These tongues of fire sat on each person in the house. Then each person was filled with God's Holy Spirit. They began to speak in different languages. The Holy Spirit helped them.

Jews from all over the world were in Jerusalem at that time. When they heard the sound of the wind, they came running. Each person heard Jesus' helpers speaking about God in his own language. It was amazing!

Then Peter stood up and told the crowd
of people the Good News about Jesus
Christ. About three thousand people
believed Peter and were baptized that day!

# Kids Life QUESTIONS

1. Where did the Holy Spirit come from?

2. What sound did the people hear when the Holy Spirit came?

3. What did the Holy Spirit make Jesus' helpers able to do?

4. Can the Holy Spirit help you tell other people about Jesus, too?

## FUN & FACTS

*Pente* is a Greek word that means *five*. It is often used with other words in the Bible. *Pentecost* in this story was *fifty* days after the Passover Feast. The *Pentateuch* is the first *five* books of the Old Testament.

# the Beautiful Gate

*Acts 3:1-10*

One day Peter and John went to the temple. It was three o'clock in the afternoon. This was the time for the daily temple prayers.

A crippled man was sitting by the temple gate. It was called the Beautiful Gate. The man had been crippled all his life. Every day he was carried there to beg. He asked people going to the temple for money.

The crippled man saw Peter and John.
He said, "Can you give a poor man a
little money, please?"

Peter and John looked straight at the
man. They said, "Look at us!" The crippled
man looked at them; he thought they were
going to give him some money.

Peter said, "We don't have any money. But we have something else we can give you. By the power of Jesus Christ, stand up and walk!" Then Peter took the man's right hand and helped him stand up.

The man's feet and ankles were strong as soon as he stood up. He went with Peter and John to the temple. He was walking and jumping and praising God!

All the people knew who the man was. They knew he was the crippled man who always sat by the gate. Now they saw him walking and jumping. They were surprised and amazed. Peter told the people that the man had been healed by the power of Jesus. Then all the people began to praise God.

# Kids Life QUESTIONS

1. Where did the crippled man sit every day?

2. What gift did Peter and John give him?

3. Who really healed the crippled man?

4. What can you do to help a crippled man?

## FUN & FACTS

The Jews had three times to pray every day. The first time each day was in the middle of the morning—about 9:00 a.m. The second time of prayer was at the time for the evening sacrifice about 3:00 p.m. The third time of prayer was at sunset each evening. Peter and John were going to the 3:00 p.m. time of prayer in this story.

# Seven Servants Chosen

*Acts 6:1-7*

More and more people were believing in Jesus, and His church was growing every day. But as the church grew, problems began to appear.

One group of Jews complained to the other group of Jews. They said their women without husbands were not getting food each day. So, Jesus' helpers called all the people together to talk.

They decided to choose seven good and wise men to take care of handing out food. That way Jesus' special helpers could keep on teaching the Good News. Everyone thought this was a good idea.

They chose these seven men: Stephen, Philip, Procorus, Nicanor, Timon, Parmenas, Nicolas. They brought these men to Jesus' helpers. The helpers placed their hands on the seven men and prayed for them. Then the church grew even faster!

# Kids Life QUESTIONS

1. What was happening to Jesus' church?

2. How many men did they choose to hand out food?

3. What were Jesus' special helpers going to do?

4. Do you know someone you could take some food to?

## FUN & FACTS

The seven men chosen to hand out food may have been the first church *deacons*. The word *deacon* means *servant*. They are people chosen to serve the church in special ways. You can read more about deacons in I Timothy 3:8-13.

# A Nobleman Is Saved

*Acts 8:26-39*

An angel of the Lord spoke to Philip. He said, "Go down the road from Jerusalem to Gaza." As Philip was going he met a man from Ethiopia. He was a very important man. He took care of the queen's money. The man had been to Jerusalem to worship. Now he was going home.

The Holy Spirit told Philip, "Go to that man's chariot and stay near it." So, Philip ran up to the chariot. He heard the man reading God's Word. Philip said, "Do you understand what you are reading?"

"No," the nobleman said. "Will you help me?"

Philip got into the chariot with the man. He started at the very same Scripture. He told the nobleman the Good News about Jesus.

As they rode along they came to some water. The nobleman wanted to be baptized. Philip and the nobleman both went down into the water. Philip baptized him. When they came up out of the water, the nobleman went on his way. He was so happy! And Philip went back to preaching.

# Kids Life QUESTIONS

1. Who told Philip to go meet the nobleman?

2. What did Philip teach the nobleman?

3. What did the nobleman want to do when they came to some water?

4. Have you ever told anyone a story from the Bible? Which story did you tell?

## FUN & FACTS

We can read any part of the Bible that we want to—either the Old or New Testament. However this Ethiopian man could only read from the Old Testament. He was reading what the book of Isaiah said about Jesus. The Holy Spirit helped Philip explain what the words meant, even though the New Testament had not even been written yet!

# Saul Meets Jesus

*Acts 9:1-22*

Saul was on his way from Jerusalem to Damascus. He was going there to put Jesus' followers in jail. He had his soldiers with him.

Suddenly, a bright light from heaven flashed around Saul. He fell to the ground. Then a voice said, "Saul, Saul, why are you hurting Me?"

Saul said, "Who are You, Lord?"

The voice said, "I am Jesus—the One you are trying to hurt."

Jesus told Saul to go into Damascus and wait. He said Saul would be told what to do. But when Saul opened his eyes, he was blind! His soldiers had to lead him by the hand into the city. Saul was blind for three days. He did not eat or drink anything.

God sent a man named Ananias to see Saul. He put his hands on Saul and said, "Saul, Jesus has sent me. You will now be able to see. You will also be filled with God's Holy Spirit."

At that very moment, Saul could see again. He was baptized and started telling others the Good News about Jesus.

# Kids Life QUESTIONS

1. Where was Saul going?

2. Why was he going to Damascus?

3. Who did Saul meet on the road?

4. Who could you tell about Jesus this week?

## FUN & FACTS

Damascus was a very important city. Traders from all over the world came there to trade their goods. Saul knew that God's Word would spread to the whole world from Damascus. He was going there to try and stop God's Word. But it did not work. Instead, God turned Saul into one of His greatest preachers!

# Dorcas Lives Again

*Acts 9:36-42*

In the city of Joppa was a woman named Dorcas. She was a follower of Jesus. She was always doing good and helping the poor. One day Dorcas became ill and died. Her friends put her in an upstairs room.

Peter was in Lydda, a town near Joppa. The friends of Dorcas sent two men to get him. They said, "Hurry, Peter! Please come with us!" Peter got dressed and went with them to Joppa.

When Peter came, they took him to the
room upstairs. The women stood
around Peter crying. They showed him
clothes Dorcas had made for them. They
were all so sad that Dorcas had died.

Peter sent everyone out of the room. He knelt down and prayed to God. Then he said to the body, "Dorcas, stand up!" Right then Dorcas opened her eyes. She saw Peter and sat up. Peter helped her to stand.

Peter called all the friends of Dorcas and Jesus' followers into the room. He showed them that Dorcas was alive! People everywhere in Joppa heard what had happened. Many people believed in Jesus.

# Kids Life QUESTIONS

1. In what town did Dorcas live?

2. Why were all the people in Joppa sad?

3. Who really raised Dorcas back to life?

4. Do you have some clothes you could give to poor people?

## FUN & FACTS

Many important things happened in the city of Joppa. It was an important seaport. This is where Jonah got on the boat when he ran away from God. This is also where Peter had a dream on a housetop. In the dream God told Peter that He loves all people the same way.

# God Saves Cornelius's Family

*Acts 10:1-48*

Cornelius was an officer in the Roman army. He lived in Caesarea. He was not a Jew. But Cornelius and all his family believed in God. He gave a lot of his money to the poor. And he prayed to God often.

One day Cornelius saw an angel. The angel said, "God has heard your prayers. He has seen your gifts to the poor. And God remembers you. Send someone to Joppa to get a man named Peter. Bring him here."

At the same time, Peter was in Joppa. He was praying on the housetop. God showed Peter a dream. The dream meant that God loves all people in the world the same—both Jews and non-Jews.

The next day Peter came to Cornelius's house. Cornelius had all his family and friends together. Peter said, "God has shown me that He loves all people the same. It does not matter to Him what country a person is from." Then Peter told them the Good News about Jesus.

Suddenly God's Holy Spirit came down on them. The Holy Spirit had been given to non-Jewish people, too! Then Cornelius and his family were baptized in the name of Jesus Christ.

# Kids Life QUESTIONS

1. Who was Cornelius?

2. Why did God want Peter to come and talk to Cornelius?

3. Does God love all people in the world the same?

4. How many different kinds of people does God love? How many can you name?

## FUN & FACTS

The Jewish people had many laws that told them the right way to live. One of these laws said that there were certain kinds of food they could not eat. Cornelius could eat these foods, and he offered them to Peter. Peter realized that it was all right for him to eat these foods. God was using this to show Peter that He loved all people.

# Paul Travels for God

*Acts 13:1-3; 14:8-15*

In the church at Antioch were many prophets and teachers. One day the Holy Spirit came to them. He said, "Give Barnabas and Paul to Me. I have a special work for them to do." The church prayed and gave up eating for a while. They blessed Barnabas and Paul and sent them on their way.

Barnabas and Paul travelled to many cities for God. Everywhere they went they told the Good News of Jesus. At last they came to a city named Lystra.

A crippled man was listening to Paul preach. He had been crippled all his life. Paul saw that this man believed God could heal him. Paul said to him, "Stand up on your feet." The man jumped up and began walking around!

The crowds of people saw what happened. They were amazed. They thought Barnabas and Paul were gods. The people shouted, "The gods have become men. They have come down to us!"

**P**riests of the false god named Zeus heard the news. They brought some bulls and flowers to the city gates. They wanted to worship Barnabas and Paul.

But Barnabas and Paul heard what the people were doing. They ran into the crowd to stop them. They said, "Why are you doing this? We are only men like you. We are not gods. We came to tell you the Good News. Turn away from these false gods. Believe in the true living God!"

T hen some Jews from Antioch turned the people against Paul. They tried to kill Paul with stones! But he got away. Paul and Barnabas left Lystra and went to the city of Derbe.

# Kids Life QUESTIONS

1. Why did the people think Barnabas and Paul were gods?

2. What were the priests going to do with the bulls and flowers?

3. Why did Barnabas and Paul stop the people from worshipping them?

4. How does God feel about people worshiping other gods but Him?

## FUN & FACTS

When Saul met Jesus, his name was changed to Paul. Paul made three trips to preach for God. They are called *missionary journeys*. Everywhere he went, Paul told the Good News about Jesus. He started many churches for Jesus. And he wrote many of the books in the New Testament.

# Jesus Will Come Again!

*Revelation 1:1-3; 21:1–22:21*

John was one of Jesus' special helpers.
One day Jesus sent an angel to John. He
gave John a wonderful message. And he
told John to write the message in a book.
The angel said, "The person who reads the
words of God's message and does what it
says will be happy."

The angel showed John many wonderful things. One thing John saw was a beautiful new city. The city was made of pure gold! And the city was sitting on jewels like sapphire, emerald, and topaz.

The city had twelve gates. Each gate was made from one great big pearl. The street of the city was made of pure gold. But you could see through the gold as if it were glass.

There was no need for the sun or moon in the city. The glory of God was so bright that there was never any night there!

A beautiful river flowed from the throne of God down the middle of the street. It was shining like crystal. The tree of life was on each side of the river. It had twelve different kinds of fruit on it!

Then Jesus said, "Listen! I am coming again very soon. My followers will go into this new city. They will drink the water of life. They will eat the fruit from the tree of life. They will live there forever!"

And John said, "Amen. Come, Lord Jesus!"

# Kids Life QUESTIONS

1. Who showed John the new city?

2. What wonderful things did John see?

3. Who will get to live in the new city?

4. Do you want to live in heaven someday, too?

## FUN & FACTS

The word *Revelation* means *uncovering*. In this book Jesus was taking the cover off something wonderful to let John see it. What John saw was the future for Jesus' followers. We will live as kings in heaven—a place made of gold and jewels! I really want to go there, don't you?